Out Of The Attic

Douglas S Johnson

1999
PROSPECT PRESS
Sistersville
West Virginia

Published by Prospect Press
609 Main Street
Sistersville, West Virginia 26175

Library of Congress Catalog Card Number: 98-067223

ISBN: 1-892668-04-1

Manufactured in the United States of America

First Edition

10 9 8 7 6 5 4 3 2 1

Dedications

To Mary, who continues to give me light and room to work.
Thanks, as always, to my family, for their ongoing encouragement.
Special thanks to Ashley, who assures me that if I can still run, I'm not old.
Also to Casey, our greyhound, who taught me not to roll over and play dead for anyone.

Table of Contents

Introduction

In the past fifteen years or so, I have written over 1,000 poems. Invariably, some of these have stood out, have been widely published and have received various kinds of acclaim, while others (many of equal or even superior quality, and so through no fault of their own) have fallen by the wayside. In **Out Of The Attic,** I wish to take the opportunity to dust off some of my "lost" verses and present them in a collected form so that, at last, they might clearly see the light of day.

Acknowledgments

Certain poems in this collection have appeared previously in **Night Songs** (audio cassette), **Treasured Poems Of America** (Sparrowgrass Publishing), The Sunday Suitor, Byline, **Footprints** (Poetry Unlimited), ? Mark, The New Times, Poetic Page, **This Is My Beloved** (Anderie Poetry Press), Poetry Plus Magazine, The Maryland Poetry Review, apostrophe, **Cats, Canines & Other Critters** (Anderie Poetry Press), Poet's Fantasy, **Summer Treasures IV** (Rio Grande Press), **With Every New Dawn** (Pig's Wing Press), **A Runner's Life** (Golden Apples Press), Avalon Rising, Wurdz, Kansas English, The Pittsburg Morning Sun, Midwest Poetry Review, **Poetic Voices Of America,** (Sparrowgrass Publishing), Spilled Ink, Touchstone, Celebration Of Oneness, and American Poets & Poetry.

"Angel At Dawn" appeared on a set of bookmarks issued by Poetry In Motion.

Out Of The Attic

I.

And now
You have gotten
Into everything:
Into morning bagels-
Into armchairs-
And into Mozart' s
Last concerto.
You have gone rummaging
Through my life
And brought back treasures.
You have found
Your way
Into my pockets-
And my cabinets-
And form little orbits
Of ecstasy
Along the rims
Of my glassware.
You linger
In my lampshades.
You hide
In my sugar bowl.

1991

Sometimes when the cherry bloom
Of your touch lights as soft
As love upon my arm,
It is too marvelous to be alive—
And the world awakens
With angels and mourning doves
And all the joyous heartbreak
Of breathing before the sun
And watching the night
Torn to frightful rags
And knowing beyond knowing
That the words you speak
That I cannot hear
Will rise and melt with the day
And take up lodging with wordless stars.

1992

An antique window moment
Opens
Unto eternity
And the moon–
And you pass within,
And go,
And stay–
And I cannot breathe,
And I cannot die.
Shadows pass
Within.
The world breathes
Inside of me
And stars bloom
Within my breast–
And you pass,
And go,
And stay–
Behind an antique window moment.

1992

How strange some souls–
Such as I–
While sifting through the sand,
Glean the rarest grains of gold
In a universe of beaches.

1992

 **A Homecoming**

With the last dozen paddle strokes,
He notes the distant thunder,
Feels the stirring of cold wings
That flutter near his shoulder,
Smiles at the rising gusts of wind
That toss the black bird skyward,
Knowing now he has beaten the storm.
Inside him grows an intangible heat,
A living, vibrating electricity
To match the mouse-like scurryings
Of lightning on the horizon.
He feels a blessed spirit come near
Who whispers like the waves,
Who speaks of the miracle of return
With the owls in nearby caves.

1994

Coming Home

I am coming home to my love
After years of absence
On a morning that began
With the press of gulls at dawn
And salty ocean tears
And which now delightfully reels
With new southern winds
And the dappled density of woods
And with young green leaves
Which push their last red forefathers
From limbs and down to me.
And then, past trees and rolling fields,
Standing there, like God's final creation,
Is that most familiar house,
And I weep, and I run
Under a vast Van Gogh sky
Full of enormous suns.

1994

 **She Picks Primroses**

She picks primroses,
Unaware of the butterfly
Perched in her hair or how
Her hands hold my heart
As we both stand here
Beneath the blue boil
Of the summer sky
And the noontide sun.

She picks primroses,
Oblivious that the universe
Is for long moments bent
About her softened features
Like the borders
Of a cameo brooch
In which she is forever
Daintily frozen.

She picks primroses,
Unaware that I am here,
Not thinking of the night
She woke me to feed me
A pomegranate seed by seed
And make love in moonlight
Or when she patched
My jeans with purple cloth.

She picks primroses,
Smiling sweetly and singing
Softly to the wind
Of the one she loves
And for whom she picks
These delicate flowers,
And sadly I know she
No longer sings for me.

1994

The Photograph

She waits, staring out
From a sepia-colored photograph
Hung in the back hallway:
A barely palm-sized three-by-five
In which she and I, then young,
Stand jauntily beneath a willow tree,
I with cap pulled tight and low
To shade what I hoped
Were the serious eyes
Of a curious genius or of a poet
Pondering a world that could produce
The likes of this one with me;
She with loose long hair
Blown wildly around her smile,
Her head turned slightly askance
While her fingers held some casual motion
That made it clear she was
Probably unaware of the camera
And of herself and of anything
But the sun and the breeze
And the everyday pleasures she hid
Like candy in the depths of her pockets.

Even before, I would lie awake
And think of how she looked
That day, how perfectly possessed

Of how she loved me more
Than I could ever imagine God
Loving all of humankind;
And now in these latter, emptied days
She has steadily taken
To haunting me in this same way again,
Gazing at me through death,
Unsettling the ground below me
Just as she did in living,
Pulling my fingertips
Toward her outstretched hand,
She who swore that if I died
First her life would be ruined
But thought little of leaving me
(Although I'm sure she found
Once she was gone and well reborn
That there was little love
Even on the other side
To match the one we once had here);
And so her spirit settled
In those fading, laughing eyes
Which still shine blue in my dreams
Like the blinding skies on that day;
And there, beneath the willow tree,
She beckons and she waits for me.

1994

A Summer Nocturne

Upon what porch did you stand
And upon what step did you linger
Long to view what faint star
And think of me?
Did you believe I might be gazing
Upon that same dim light
And that all lovers
Likewise paused upon this night
And that a million mighty arcs
Were stretched through dark heaven,
To weave a God of love
Out of silver threads?
Into what bed did you retire
Beneath sheets of bold blue moonlight
And what names did silence give
And what dreams appeared
And burned like another life
In which you would gladly live?

1994

❧ Requital

For years you kept me
Like a child holds
A cookie in her palm:
Without thinking,
But with infinite care,
Placing me in your pocket
Like a string and top,
A gyroscopic toy
Which you now take out
And marvel at,
Laughing with joy
At "this is mine;
This is mine..."

1994

 **Exordium**

Your gaze absorbs
The years of absence
As your merest touch
Melts the long days lost–
As we stand wordless,
Monuments to ourselves
And to our enduring love;
We are as fountains
Of water pouring forth
 And then falling back
Into each other,
And we find etched
Into each other's hands
 An eternity of chances.

1994

The Ice Cream Man

He rolls up our street and tinny,
Tottering tunes spill into the summer air
And children fill the yards
(Swooping down from trees),
And careen about like
Circling crows with crooked smiles
To descend upon this hook-backed man
With the tiny sparrow eyes.
I come behind you on the porch,
Listening to the silence
Between the blurry, whining notes,
And hear their hidden song
The same way I listen to your heartbeats
At night (hearing only the noiseless ones)
Or watch our children and note
The invisible motions
Just before–and just after–
As they take wing and fly
From the hardwood porch
Across the fresh-mown lawn
To join in rapturous whirlings
The widening gyre of ravens.
I take your elbow with my hand
And laugh aloud to think I am
Living in this place and loving you
Here during all the moments in between.

1994

 **Making Plans**

On the night after the quake
Briefly shook our tucked away town,
In the wake of the last faint
Rumblings of aftershock,
You turn a bit in my arms,
Then solemnly start to write
Your plans for our future
In the flesh of my back
With the tip of your finger,
Assured that if your words
Reach down and linger in my blood
That I will have no choice
Except to live long enough
To see them unfold and bloom
Like your flowerbeds of roses.

1994

ᴄ⁓ Parallax

Now, as I stand upon this bridge,
 A lock of your red hair,
Aflame, falls from my fingers,
Racing into the waiting water below,
A strange, sibilant firework,
A teardrop of light on a starless night
Oddly out of sync with the time
When first I touched your fiery curls;
And here in the dark I remember once more
How years before they fell so softly, slowly
About your face and shoulders,
Tossed about by loving summer winds
As you stood in waist-high waving grasses
Beneath the shadows of moving clouds
During the days when we still loved.

1994

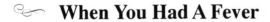 # When You Had A Fever

I smoothed your brow and dabbed
Your cheeks with an icy cloth,
And closed your eyes with kisses,
Then opened them again to spoon
You a simple, watery broth,
And laid in bed with you and felt
Your body's burning heat upon my limbs,
As silently you slept once more
Beneath the freshly laundered sheets,
I ready to die for peacefulness,
Knowing I had purchased at the store
Meat, and carrots, and onions–all
Of which would make a hearty soup
In which a crust of bread would soak,
A heavenly repast for two in love
To dine upon when your fever broke.

1995

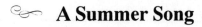 # A Summer Song

I felt your hand touch mine
Beneath the pillow as I slept,
And dreamt of those two hands,
How fingers locked as we strolled
Along the summer sands, waves
Whispering our names as fiddler
Crabs stumbled in and out
Of water like weary, drunken
Sailors near the end of leave;
And this was perfect peace to me,
The sea and two hands laced together:
All the world a laughable cup
Of sparkling wind, sunshine and sky
Stretching away and away into endless
Bliss borne of your proximity.

1995

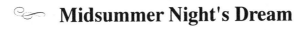 **Midsummer Night's Dream**

Tonight I'll stand on my front porch
And hurl you a comet,
A fiery ball that you may take
And do with as you please:
Become a wizardess, a *wunderfrau,*
Create a new life with it,
Something the world has never seen;
Paint your windows with its crystals;
Smear its sparkles on the lintels;
Or hold it in your belly
And relish its warmth...
Yes, this last thing most of all...

1996

Verse Written In Age For A Young Woman

Who's never seen thee, never lived:
The dawn's light sparkles, softly hived
In Spring's young leaves above your head
As you stray 'midst the flower bed;
Gay girl of budding breasts, and eyes
Of virgin blue, and unsighed sighs:
I watch you through the lawn* of age
Which closes 'fore sight's window pane,
Though not enough to hide thy form
Moving within my night, thy morn;
How can a man as I love you?
Can cold December love the dew?
Can May love snow, or hot July
Welcome ice, or fair April lie
In downy beds with old November?
(Nay, June hardly Janus remembers.)
The world, it never has run so;
Thy noon's not come; my star won't go
Back to day's break, where it begun
(That we might shine as double suns.)
Then let us meet in some other world,
Some other time, unsprung, yet coiled
Within the works of untold fate,
Each hour make full, each minute sate:
If God, prithee, helps me recall

In Spring, the wisdom of the Fall
And let in me the Summer's heat
With Winter's patience, my love meet.

*lawn: transparent fabric used for curtains

1997

II.

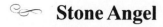 **Stone Angel**

In an ancient cathedral,
A stone angel watches,
Her eyes cast upward
As she leans outward,
Straining from her perch
And reaching toward heaven,
Begging God to take her
From this place which falls
About her feet, crumbles
Daily, abandoned, unused
By the forgetful heathens who
Have not the wisdom or will
To sustain or to destroy.

1995

Angel At Dawn

Stone statue
Receiving the rain
With upturned palms,
Gazing downward
Through filtered light
As another autumn
Morning bleeds through
Clouds and the dead
Rise in mists to
Gather at her feet:
Faint rays limn
The marbles, issue
From her fingertips.

1995

What I Saw

A pear fell from the tree
Behind you as you walked
Through the far orchard:
When you turned to look
I saw that in your smile
There were all the words
Ever spoken on the earth.

1995

25

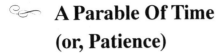 **A Parable Of Time
(or, Patience)**

Alone, you throw
Cold, rounded stones
Into the ocean's swell,
Watching them sink,
Disappear, in the hiss
Of great gray waves--
Are you amazed
When they are borne
Back to you, when
They roll in sunlight
And shine at your feet?

1996

 **Darshan**

This morning,
I moved to my window,
Stretched forth my arms,
And from my fingers
Fell oranges (round
And sweet as a young
Girl's breasts)
And bright candies
(Spraying like fireworks)
As children gathered
In the street below
And received the gift.

Just before I turned
Back to my upstairs room,
I smiled, noticing
That the sun glowed
Like God's eye
In the palm of my left hand.
So I threw that
Down to them too.

1997

We stand in vast and spreading fields,
In astonishments of grass:
Ourselves an inch of earthly *know*
In acres of *perhaps.*

1997

III.

The Little Dead

The little dead mole
That the dogs drug about
Like a bit of rag
Not an hour ago
Lies on the faded blue carpet
In a corner of the garage.
He is no bigger
Than a mouse, really;
And from here he seems
Comfortably asleep.
Perhaps it was one
Of the cats
That brought him here,
Who stole his life
And sold his dignity
To a frivolous pack of pups.
I can imagine the hopeless
Pas de deux
He danced with the tabby,
The graceful *pas de chat*
Of his crucifier
As she daintily ended
His living.

Do the little dead die
Any easier,
With any less agony,
With fewer frantic scrambles
For a life which slips away
Like water through
A worn-out sieve?
What honor has this
Little roll of rumpled rags
Ever known?
And now, out
With the morning garbage.

1986

 **Desert Snail**

Rain for you
Is a harbinger of living,
And the loving hands
Of the raindrops
Caress your crusty back
Like the love
Of a good woman.
You are as solitary
As grieving children,
As lonely as the washing
Ebb and flow
Of eternal spaces.
The gentle rains
Are as seldom as stars,
And the nights are black
And as full of nothingness
As a businessman's mind.

1987

The Neighbor

I slept halfway in the hall that night,
So you might feel me near--or I might hear
Your fading heartbeat there in the floorboards,
Or so I, who cared more for them, might catch
The fallen stitches of past years
Full of nervous yapping dogs,
The harsh white light of naked bulbs,
And the glints from a single set of silver
Carefully washed each night at six;
Or perhaps to finally resolve your face
Which became unfocused in recent days
And then unraveled, fell away.

And one by one, the gems and stones
Of your waning life gathered round me
There in the airless dark:
Shorn hopes, unopened doors, fragments of
                                    bones;
And by midnight I knew you well enough
That I didn't even flinch
When I heard the sharp pop of the pistol
And the final trembling in the boards.

1994

We must earn our Death
From Life: going down
Into the sooty depths of
Airless caves, emerging
With gems, round and blue,
Like the eyes of Russian
Girls; we send a burning
Life skyward in yellow curls
Of smoke, a divine holocaust;
We dare to save even those
Who do not desire saving,
Forcing their blind faces
Toward the searing sun so
They cannot help but see
The brooding, multiplying
Orbs that gaze from endless
Dimensions of possibility.

1995

you are perched upon a spindle at
this very moment: wheeling
on its pinpoint,
  the
world whipping by like a mad video
locked on fast forward

you turn

through the winds of demon
    laughter,
through the tactile beckonings
    into the fingers that crook

and tempting orbs that promise
from every possible direction,
listening for a thin and straining
voice you pray persists

one final time, you cast
your eyes about,
all of eternity to lose:
    now, fool,
plant a foot and choose

1995

For A Breech-Born Guinea Pig

The sun parrots have flown
From the murdered Amazon;
The loamy mind of the earth
Is stultified in cement;
And all the while, hope
Vanishes faster than all the rest--
But what of the curly-haired rodent
I pulled by the feet from his mother's
Womb this morning before breakfast?
What of the way it kicked and cried
And bumbled about?
What of its first awkward munchings
At fresh lettuce?
What of it asleep at its mother's
Side, both worn and weary after
The struggle toward life and breathing?
 What of that?

1996

 **Rachel's Children**

Do not weep.
We are as buckets of pure water,
Drawn upward from darkness
Into the red light of a setting sun.
We are as stones, hurled from a sling,
Moving fiercely through the night
Toward unseen targets.
We are as summer constellations
In winter, turned from sight,
But never lost, gleaming elsewhere,
Shining on deserts and generations
Of men not yet born unto the earth.
We are as books whose pages
Have not yet been written, which wait
In Holy silence, pure and whole,
Patient as the ocean's deepest deep.
We are not dead, but ever living;
So, dear mother of our tribe,
Do not weep.

1997

For Anne Frank

With hands still trembling
With innocence and stained
By the Keatsean pallor
Of a famished fledgling ardor,
You grasped a fountain pen,
                a hundred books,
                a wire fence,
                a million lives--
And still you will not stop,
Grasping, clutching at us all
When we are trying to sleep,
Winding your bony, ringed finger
Into our freshly-washed hair.
Like the ghost of a dead daughter
We never wanted or knew we had,
You draw us back by the hand
Just as we are driving ourselves
Down into the oblivion of dark;
You will not let us go, you will
Not let us free of ourselves;
You, my lost girl, are ruthless,
A crooked-toothed tormentor.

1997

IV.

Poem For Piano, Flute And Voice

Hands playing,
Hands playing,
Hands playing keys:
Whose hands are these?
Whose hands are these
Playing these keys?
Lips playing,
Lips playing
Lips playing pipes:
Whose hands are these?
Whose hands are these
Playing these keys?
Whose lips are these?
Whose lips are these
Playing these pipes?
Tongues tonguing
Tongues tonguing
Tongues tonguing songs:
Whose hands are these?
Whose hands are these
Playing these keys?
Whose lips are these?
Whose lips are these

Playing these pipes?
Whose tongues are these?
Whose tongues are these
Tonguing these songs?

1986

September

September's strong, seductive fingers
Slide slowly along her sides--
He sends slow breaths
Along her flesh
While loosening the roughened wormwood
Of Summer's smoldering brassiere.

He gets this way with her every year--
So her blushes,
Her at-first coy reluctance,
Seem superfluous at best.
But–as always–at last–
She brings forth broad hips,
Struggling out of weathered silks.
She boldly allows bronzed bared breasts
To accept his caressing breeze.

And then he lovingly strokes
The last wet blackberries
From the niches of her thighs–
She sighs the last wet grasses–
He coaxes sweet, small strawberries
That come shivering
From her breasts–
They pull the last black leaves

From the tops of the cherry trees
In the trial of their terrible embraces.

The sun turns away–aloof and discreet–
But does it very slow.
He knows
The faint hues of her smile–
That cock of her knee.

1992

 **Generations III**

He got so good at it over time,
We hardly ever heard him
As he labored with rowing each day
In the bowels of the sturdy framework
Of our taut-rigged family which sailed
In this dark, vast ocean of uncertainty
While others sank, or ran aground
Or were abandoned to a violent storm.
Through it all, his firm, sure motions
Moved us through steady currents
Which were forever against him;
And though, often enough, we went below
And saw how it was he worked for us,
It was very rare we saw it as such;
And whenever we did come before him,
Our Captain and self-imprisoned slave,
It was usually only to beg *his* praise
Or to tell him a blow had come up
And to ask, could he row a bit harder?
I no longer wonder why he rarely spoke,
But I wonder how he was always able,
No matter what, to muster one stroke more–

And now–I–praying my arms are half as

                                strong,

Sit down to the oars
And place my unsure fingers
To handles his grip wore smooth.

1994

Two Friends

I.

We stand looking
Out over the land
Stretched before us
Like an opened palm,
At our children's children
And infinite generations
Playing untold games
In the valley of our lives.

II.

We are at once amazed
One night by the heft
And raw muscularity
Of our love,
How it is in the blood
And the limbs
And the motions
Of all those who came after.

III.

There is something of us
In all future time
As there was a trace
Of our being
And of our being together
In the sharp glints of light
Upon the surface
Of ancient streams,
And in the sad strange look
Of all the world's strangers
Who grew tired of living,
And in Whitman's
Great guffaw of laughter.

IV.

We are the fountains
Of earthly things,
Willows finding glory
In lost leaves,
Forever living
Through our falling away.

V.

We are pleased
With our own eternity,
With God's durability
Woven into our fibers
With wild daisy chains
Of love and letting go–
And letting go.

VI.

It is no wonder
Children drop pebbles
Down deep wells–
It is to hear the far-away answer.

1994

Bonsai

Inverted umbrella,
Supporting the whole
Trembling universe
There in the bowl
Of your fragrant branches,
Cradle my life also:
Balance it for me
In moments when I
Seem rather than be.
We shall mend together:
I will trim and bend
Your bowers, and you
Will shelter me there
In delicate structure
When this wicked world
Defies all shape or sense.

1996

Bonsai II

I trim my little bonsai,
Not certain where my knees
Begin and the earth ends,
Unsure whether I breathe
The air or if it breathes me,
Often losing my wandering
Fingers in the branches
Of my tiny, reaching tree.
What is me, and what is other?
And what does it matter?

1996

V.

Rain, my benevolent lover,
Cups my life in hands
More delicate than death
And opens unto me
A way to full existence
And becomes a source
Of graceful knowing,
A how to fall
When falling is living
Itself;
And a how to run
When forward motion
Is my only hymn to God;
A solitude,
And solemn voice
Of man's short summer;
A teacher of dying in falling, in living
Itself .

1992

My feet fall
And strike the ground,
Pure speed and sound,
Like August plums
Turning loose of trees.
I am absolved
By summer's end,
Made holy
By past striving,
All surmounted hills
Stored in a heart
Strained
Of its own
Strange desire.

1992

I am a Runner–
God's Lonely Man–
A castaway
In athlete's clothes,
Propped by invisible
Arms,
With the scent
Of snow
Forever in my nose
And a searing heat
Forever at my shoulder,
A divine vagabond
Pulled forward
By Spring
And pushing
Against the World
With legs that cut quick
Harps into the unforgiving
Autumnal air.

1992

Perhaps it is to outrun
Myself–
Or God–
Or to pursue us both–
To outdo angst
In its dirty deeds
Of restlessness
And endless locomotion.
Perhaps this is why
My feet burn
And my limbs boil
When I stand still.

1992

VI.

 **Leaving Pittsburg, Kansas**

First I wonder
If I'll ever feel again
Beneath my feet
The round, knobby corners
Of hard-worn bricks
In cobblestone streets
Or if again
I'll ever be stirred
By a sound nearly as sweet
As that
Of the bold brass bell
In the tower of St. Mary's
As it rang in six o'clock
On an April evening.
And now what
Will I ever find
To replace the sorrowful face
Of the lonely angel
That hovers over
Her abandoned company
Of long forgotten spirits
In the cemetery
On the far edge of town?

How far down can I push
Such things
In my memory
Before they surface
Once more
Like strange dark fish
Struggling toward
The surface of the sea?

As we rumble away
From our home
In that lumbering Ryder
Stuffed full of memories
And bits of clay,
I find I am in love
With the whirling fan
In the front window
Of Jackson's Electric.
I want to get out
And tell it goodbye
And run my fingers
Once more
Over the rough red brick
Of the Stillwell Hotel
Which continues to crumble
To bits and fall
Onto the flat black roof
Of Otto's Cafe.

To turn around and stay
Would only prove
That my blood is in the soil,
That I couldn't live without
The day-to-day lime green
Of Ettinger's Office Supply.
I try not to look back
At the century-old monoliths
That are the Fox Theatre
And the Gutteridge Pharmacy
(But do anyway–)
I say these names
Over and over
Like an incantation
And then listen one last time
To the harsh scrape
Of a woman's shoes
On square stones.
All the sacred blood
In a deep-stained sky
Cannot atone
For the lost wailing of trains
Or for that of the stone angel
Which will weep
To see me leave
To return no more.

1993

Train-Haunted Land

Train-haunted land,
I have left you–
Left you
Like some sort
Of a gallant fool
Perched upon a horse
And unable to smell
My own blood
In the soil.

I knew not then
I would awaken
With your wailing
Whistle
Blowing through
My brain,
Or that the wild,
Time-hungry pistons
Would be lodged
In the valves
Of my midnight heart,
Or that their flailing
Rhythm would launch
My blood
Through my limbs
In the dark
In this strange land.

I didn't know
The blowing grass,
Moved by a million
Careful fingertips,
Would fill my dreams
And whisper strange names,
Or that the wind-tangled trees
Would reach down
To clutch at my hand
After I was already
Too far away.

Too soon the dawn returns,
And the pistons fade
To grey,
And then are gone–
And the grasses
Are stilled,
And all the strange names
Fall away–
And your faint whistle
Calls to me,
Dopplerwise,
And then wraps itself
In Night.

Train-haunted land,
I have left you.

1993

Washington Song

Crouched in the hollow bone of a heron's wing,
I know the heft of silvered skies
As we fly–bird and I–over Western evergreens
Through which the sun's rare yellow blooming gleam
Is like the sudden unshuttering of a stranger's eye
(When it bothers to be seen.)
Now above the lusty fragrance of new tulips
And over the coy forsythia's faint seduction,
I smell your apple-scented hair
And I know that you are somewhere
Here in this pewter dawn
Waiting for me–with circling swallows-
In a high-grown meadow
Wet with the interminable rain.
After pain of absence, my soaking
Fingers melt in yours
(Like scattered drops on window panes–)
Already rain presses our hair
And even now blurs our faces in shades of grey–

I shake myself free–fall from heaven
Into your land, your soul,
And lie with you in dripping acres of love.

1993

Western Song
(for Ruthie)

I have traveled the land of my soul–
I have seen the mountains of my own mind–
I have sprung from the shimmering chrysalis
        of my own captivity
Into new, brave lights of joy.
I have found my new Jerusalem
Amidst a vast wreckage of Babylons–
I have emerged from the narrow caves
        of disbelief
Into the sun of truth mirrored by a
        thousand ages–
I sink like roots into living
As though for the first time,
And feel the terror and the joy of my
        own pulse
In a land of beauty and light.

1993

VII.
(Three Poems For
A Guinea Pig Named Ruthie)*
Ruthie's Glasses

I look foreign in my glasses–
It does not seem like me.
But when I take my glasses off,
I cannot see to see.

1996

Ruthie's Big Toe

My big toe is a loner–
The others think it queer.
I use it most for scratching
Behind my itchy ear.

1996

Ruthie's Big Problem

My problem is they're rudders
For some enormous barge–
Without these ears, I cannot hear,
But why are they so large?

1996
* Drawings By Mary A. Johnson

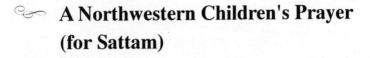

A Northwestern Children's Prayer (for Sattam)

Now I lay me down to sleep;
Lord, bless me now,
For pity's sake–
And if I die
In a midnight quake ...
On second thought,
Keep me awake.

1996

VIII.

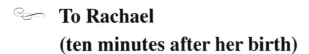

To Rachael
(ten minutes after her birth)

Little squirmy
Wormy thing
With apoplectic
Purple features,
Screaming bloody hell
To all the world,
You little
Earth grub
There wallowing
In perfectly good
Clean sheets:
You will not be
As such forever,
Or even for
Very long.
Soon enough
You will grow
Psychedelic
Butterfly wings
And fly where none
Have gone before
And where none

Shall ever
fly again.
You shall not hear
Me making
Little gurgle
Gitchy-gitchy
Goo-goo sounds,
So do not listen
For them from me.
I shall be
Waiting
For the wings
To grow.
I shall be there
When you first
Stretch
And hit the wind.

1987

☙ Ashley

Ashley, make and bake your bread
In loaves, to feed the ducklings
At the Cove, and mix in lots of Ashley love,
Along with dots of pumpkin seed,
Then knead in just compassion, finger
In your smile, then linger over
One more kneading in of laughter
For our weary world to nibble after.

1996

↝ Tony

You're Ash's brother but love dirt better,
You're something of a real go-getter–
That is, if gettin' in trouble counts
(And a peck of trouble beats an ounce.)
But still you charms us as you grows
(Something about your crinkled nose.)
Someday you'll outsmart all the guys
(Or just throw somethin' in their eyes ...)
You'll buy the world and never sell
You'll be a rough and tumble soldier
You'll give 'em fire, you'll give 'em ... well
(Let's just say "heck" until you're older.)

1996

Joe

And now we come to Joe Delizo:
Learning for him is such a breeze, oh
He's already sat and thought at college
And memorized his Book Of Knowledge.
While other guys' heads are weary,
He's tellin' all about Einstein's theory.
We're certain that he'll be successful
'Cause he's our sandbox intellectual.
Now Joe, you'll show 'em all one day
By explaining something like DNA.
For now, if big boys prove a strain,
Push them down with your giant brain.
You'll learn every language on the shelf,
And make up three or four yourself.
It's quite apparent there ain't been befo'
Another boy like this one named Joe.

1996

IX.

 Four In Imitation Of Dickinson

Its moment makes it beautiful–
It lives because it dies–
Torpid as we're waking–
And while we sleep–it flies

1990

I saw God the other day–
Out the corner of my eye–
Standing alone, and trembling–
His rosy-colored fingers twitched–
A morning song.

1990

And then again falls the shade–
The long and narrow angles of the dark
Which creep into my yard
With the mists of an airy death.
And then I know
It's come again–
My unholy, unwelcome guest.

1990

To know the time–
To know the end–
To know the why–
And then to rend
Oneself from life–
And–like a parting leaf–
                    descend

1990

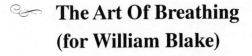

The Art Of Breathing
(for William Blake)

Teach to me the art of breathing,
Lamb whose breath comes without knowing–
Teach to me the art of being,
Joyous Piper whose soft songs
Bloom from his reed
Before he has thought
To place it to his lips–
Teach me to sing the song of life,
Sweet child who sings before speaking-
Teach me to breathe & be & sing
Like a bird who concentrates
His soul in each soft, sweet note,
Knowing nothing of music.

1993

Entelechy (after Rilke)

As we meet in this garden
Beneath the summer's fiery sun,
Listen to these pulse beats
Within my hand, loved one
And know that for you,
Blood is moving round,
That tidal floods of life
And light and sound
Strain their worn conduits
For you and for this moment,
After which the world will dream itself
Into yet another form.
Hear what this reborn flesh
Impatiently longs to tell you
Before falling away once more.
Heed the failing voice
Of blood that remembers
And longs for return;
And fear not for my death,
For I grow into you like a vine;
Rather look upon time, upon the seasons,
And then upon our loving here,
As life implodes upon itself
And then, fountainwise,
Rises, joyous, again.

1994

An Imitation Of Whitman

The ghost stroke of your hand
Against my hirsute cheek,
Your tender woman fingers
Running through my beard,
At once awakens me to darkness
And to a lonely hiss of silence,
And I caress the remains of dreams,
Praying I might linger long enough
To touch your flame-red hair,
Though my fingers fret but empty air.

1995

An Imitation Of Roethke

I knew a woman, bless her bones,
Who cracked my neck and rubbed my toes
And made me tea and buttered bread
And fluffed the pillows for my head.

She took me down and propped me up
And gave me cream for my coffee cup;
She soothed my days, and oh, my nights:
She was a soup bowl of delights.

She brought me stones and helped me sleep,
And had a white dove's lowly peep
But boy, that bird, when we got down,
Left dusty feathers on the ground

And spanked me with her big left wing
And cackled like a poultry thing;
Her lovely neck (how I was blest!)
Left me hungry for a thigh and breast.

1995

Note To His Lover
(after Li Po)

Sometimes I awaken
And check my heartbeat
Against my waiting,
Measuring time spent
Far from you in pints
Of blood and strain
On swollen arteries.
There are invisible seas
Of circumstance that
Separate us, as wide
And deep as any ocean.

1996

Botanica
(An Imitation Of Donne)

You bend to pick an ochre flower
From curvéd limb of 'suckle bower;
Yet I beg thee, to hold thy hand
And sunder not life's gentle band:
The likes that hold the bloom to limb
Doth hold the heart to breast of him
Who loves you, and espies you now
Poised here as petals on yon bough,
Lest you collect a heart and take
It with you in your apron's break;
And then, upon some helf at home
You give to it a trophy's tomb,
With no more rites than those you give
To broken shell or dried up hive.
Hearts and curios die the same,
By dust and cracks and tarnished fame:
You keep me best, and best alive
By leaving *striven* always *strive:*
Take quick the 'fume; leave else to luck:
Stoop soft to smell, but ne'er to pluck.

1997

Love Song Writ To A Mormon (after John Davies' "The Author, Loving These Homely Meats...")

If there were, oh! an ocean of coffee,*
When it cooled, Mormon mistress, I would swim
In its dun waters, all the while lofty
With the chin, not to taste of droplets dim;
No, not if it hailed sugar or rained cream,
Nor if a demon came and made it tea
And Sir Philip** swam toward me in the stream;
Nor even if the tasty Arab bean
Stained the waters green and dyed me more:
No, I would not taint my palate's virtue
For I would think of you, upon the shore,
You, Mormon mistress, caffeine-free and true.
And then, at last, my love, my thirst to cop,***
I'd drink you down, good to the lastest drop.

1997

* Mormons are forbidden the consumption of
   caffeinated potables
** *Sir Philip Sidney* (1554-1586) poet and tea
   lover
*** *cop* to take away

X.

 **Immanental Still Life**

It is replete with meaning—
The glint in a woman's eyes
When she glances up
From some thoughtful task
And faintly smiles
While her vision adjusts
Once more to the world.
It is that moment
In which she is still
Half far-away, half near,
When she is most beautiful.
It is in these scant seconds
When she sweeps like a bird
Of magnificent grace
Toward the earth,
Falling fluently through
The splendorous tangle
Of sunlit leaves.

1993

✍ A Song Of Ascents

Listen: We are alive.

No more days spent
Holding our breath
Or clenching dimes
In sweaty palms,
Caught endlessly
In a fiery Babylon
And drawn down
Into an earthquake
Of screaming voices,
Into the wide-split
Searing wounds
From which issue
Terrible sound
Turned to visible
Flame–no more
The disappearing
And disappearing,
And no more
The violent twisting
Through the febrile
Crowds: turn away
And fall upon
The ground, and
Devour fistfuls

Of grass and leaves.
Taste God in the blades.
Know the bitter grace,
And the acid power,
And the joy untold
And untellable.

1993

❧ Casualty

He stood, fiery hair blown back
And blended with the Saigon sun,
His bold blue eyes now fixed and gazing
As though confronted by distant clots
Of inane hours and wasted deeds
As Death, like a giant ancient fish,
Rose and unsettled
The marshy mud beneath his feet.

He was at first affronted,
Frightened at the prospect of this loss,
But as his ivory lids,
Softly as the hand of God,
Closed over the dazed and dazzling orbs
Of his shining eyes,
And as his vision was turned inward
And was held steadily poised
Like a gun upon himself,
He slowly embraced the bullet,
Stroked the pain like a lover,
And treasured the quaking in his limbs
Like jewels.

1993

Mountain

It is a time of revelation:
Those hours spent
In the harsh and difficult task
Of loving.

It is an ascending
Of scabrous cliffs and fluted edges,
A holding tight
To air and to the narrowest
Of fissures.

It is a severing from old ground,
From dry sand and malleable clay,
From the watery marshes of the everyday,
To give oneself utterly
To climbing,

To the mountain itself,
And to the impassive crags.
It is a joining of oneself
With stone,

Until reaching its top,
One plunges to its deepest heart,
Collapsing, wordless, into the light
Of a million suns.

1993

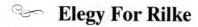

Elegy For Rilke

It is the only struggle,
This mad wrestling with angels
Here upon the dust,
The insane attempts
To pinion immortal beings
Amid the stones and shards of glass,
To find their blurry silhouettes
Where no flower will grow
And where wide masses of men
Walk in stark anonymity.

1993

 **A Song To One's Wife**

It is good to live in tragic days,
And that we carefully make our bed
In the midst of a complicated world,
And know the frailty of another day.

Thus we feel each moment complete,
A brilliant gold ring upon the hand
With all its lovely heft and gleam,
An endless orbit of actuality.

In the meadow, a swallow swings
                                  round me
In shining, widening halos,
And this instant is meaning enough.

Bend blessed circles around it,
                            dear God–
Bend blessed circles around it.

1994

 # The Communicant

If, after death, I can remain
Alive in these unleavened wafers,
And if, by chance, some stray soul
Stops and breaks a bit of me
And partakes of a true communion–
Then I, consumed, mancipated
In another's living flesh,
Am the one most truly blessed–
The revelation, the salvation

                         are mine.

1994

About The Author:

Douglas S Johnson is a writing instructor at Green River College in Auburn, Washington. He is also a Therapist/Tutor for Autistic and learning disabled children. He is the author of two other books, **Transformations** (Guyasuta Publishing) and **Between Earth And Angels** (Sterling House). He is a regularly contributing newspaper columnist and book reviewer for **The New Times**, Seattle, Washington, and writes a poetry column for **apostrophe**. Johnson places articles in a wide variety of literary magazines and educational journals and has worked as a textbook reviewer for McGraw-Hill Publishing. He has twice appeared in *Who's Who Among American Teachers*. He is a two-time winner of Sparrowgrass Publishing's National Grand Prize for poetry and has served as a judge for numerous poetry contests. His work has been praised by such poets as Ted Hughes, James Merrill and Tess Gallagher. Johnson lives in Orting, Washington, with his wife, Mary, a retired racing greyhound named Casey, five guinea pigs, Sophie, Frankie, Daisy, Dandy and Walt, a gerbil, Sam II, and Newt Rockney.